75

I am a child of

GOD

My name is

_____

PLACE
YOUR
PICTURE
HERE

Little Folded Hands

PRAYERS FOR CHILDREN

Revised by Allan Jahsmann
Illustrated by Frances Hook

Concordia Publishing House, St. Louis, Missouri

Morning Prayers

1. Dear Savior, for another night
    Of quiet sleep and rest,
    For all the joys of morning light
    Thy holy name be blest. Amen

2. For this new morning and its light,
    For rest and shelter of the night,
    For health and food, for love and friends,
    For everything Your goodness sends
    I thank You heavenly Father. Amen.

3. Oh, help me, Lord, this day to be
    Thine own dear child, to follow Thee;
    And lead me, Savior, by Thy hand
    Until I reach the heav'nly land. Amen.

4. Jesus, gentle Shepherd,
   Bless Thy lamb today;
   Keep me in Thy footsteps,
   Never let me stray.

   Guard me through the daytime,
   Every hour, I pray;
   Keep my feet from straying
   From the narrow way. Amen.

5. The morning bright
   With rosy light
   Has waked me from my sleep;
   Dear God, Thy own
   Great love alone
   Thy little one doth keep.

   All through the day,
   I humbly pray,
   Be Thou my Guard and Guide;
   My sins forgive,
   And let me live,
   Blest Jesus, near Thy side. Amen.

6. Teach me to love,
   Teach me to pray,
   Jesus above,
   Teach me Thy way.

   Tell me how I,
   In my small way,
   Can, with Thy help,
   Do good each day. Amen.

7. I thank Thee, Lord, for quiet rest.
   And for Thy care of me;
   Oh, let me through this day be blest
   And kept from harm by Thee. Amen.

8. Jesus, help me all this day
   In my work and in my play
   Both to love and to obey. Amen.

9. I thank You, Jesus, for the night
   And for the pleasant morning light,
   For rest and food and loving care
   And all that makes the world so fair.

   Help me to do the things I should,
   To be to others kind and good,
   In all I do at work or play,
   To grow more loving every day. Amen.

10. Jesus, lead me day by day
    Ever in Thine own sweet way;
    Help me to be kind and true,
    Show me what I ought to do. Amen.

11. Heavenly Father, hear my prayer;
    Keep me in Thy loving care.
    Guard me through the coming day
    In my work and in my play.
    Keep me pure and strong and true;
    Help me, Lord, Thy will to do. Amen.

12. Jesus, from Thy throne on high,
Far above the bright blue sky,
Look on us with loving eye;
Hear us, holy Jesus!

Be Thou with us every day
In our work and in our play,
When we learn and when we pray;
Hear us, holy Jesus! Amen.

13. O blessed Lord, protect Thou me
And my dear parents graciously;
From sin defend and keep me free;
Help me a Christlike child to be. Amen.

14. Dear God, my heavenly Father,
Bless me at school today,
And help me learn my lessons;
In Jesus' name I pray. Amen.

15. Loving Jesus, meek and mild,
Look upon this little child!
Make me gentle as Thou art,
Come and live within my heart.

Take my little hand in Thine,
Guide these little feet of mine.
So shall all my happy days
Be a pleasant song of praise. Amen.

16. I thank Thee, my heavenly Father, through
Jesus Christ, Thy dear Son, that Thou hast
kept me this night from all harm and danger;
and I pray Thee that Thou wouldst keep me
this day also from sin and every evil, that
all my doings and life may please Thee. For
into Thy hands I commend myself, my body
and soul, and all things. Let Thy holy angel
be with me, that the wicked Foe may have
no power over me. Amen.

Evening Prayers

17.   Dear Jesus, bless me tonight. Amen.

18.   Jesus, lay Your hand on me;
        Bless me, and take care of me. Amen.

19.   Watch o'er this little child tonight,
        Blest Savior from above,
        And keep me till the morning light
        Within Thine arms of love. Amen.

20.   Forgive, O Lord, through Thy dear Son,
        The wrongs that I this day have done;
        That with the world, myself, and Thee
        I, when I sleep, at peace may be. Amen.

21. Dear Father in heaven,
    Look down from above;
    Bless daddy and mommy,
    And all whom I love.

    May angels guard over
    My slumbers, and when
    The morning is breaking,
    Awake me. Amen.

22. Now I lay me down to sleep;
    I pray Thee, Lord, Thy child to keep;
    When in the morning I awake
    Help me the path of love to take,
    And this I ask for Jesus' sake. Amen.

23. Now I lay me down to sleep;
    I pray Thee, Lord, my soul to keep.
    If I should die before I wake,
    I pray Thee, Lord, my soul to take;
    And this I ask for Jesus' sake. Amen.

24. The day is done;
O God the Son,
Look down upon
Thy little one!

O Light of light,
Keep me this night,
And send to me
Thy presence bright.

I need not fear
If Thou art near;
Thou art my Savior
Kind and dear. Amen.

25. Be near me, Lord Jesus!
I ask Thee to stay
Close by me forever
And love me, I pray.
Bless all the dear children
In Thy tender care,
And take us to heaven
To live with Thee there. Amen.

26. Now the light has gone away;
    Savior, listen while I pray,
    Asking Thee to watch and keep
    And to send me quiet sleep.

    Jesus, Savior, wash away
    All that has been wrong today;
    Help me every day to be
    Good and gentle, more like Thee.

    Let my near and dear ones be
    Always near and dear to Thee.
    Oh, bring me and all I love
    To Thy happy home above. Amen.

27. At the close of every day,
    Lord, to Thee, I kneel and pray.
    Look upon Thy little child,
    Look in love and mercy mild;
    Please forgive and wash away
    All my naughtiness this day;
    While I sleep and when awake,
    Bless me for my Savior's sake. Amen.

28. Jesus, tender Shepherd, hear me,
Bless Thy little lamb tonight;
Through the darkness be Thou near me,
Keep me safe till morning light.

All this day Thy hand has led me,
And I thank Thee for Thy care;
Thou hast warmed and clothed and fed me;
Listen to my evening prayer.

May my sins be all forgiven;
Bless the friends I love so well;
Take us all at last to heaven,
Happy there with Thee to dwell. Amen.

29. Dear Father, whom I cannot see,
Smile down from heaven on little me.

Let angels through the darkness spread
Their holy wings around my bed.

And keep me safe, because I am
My loving Shepherd's little lamb. Amen.

30. Good night, Lord Jesus,
Guard us in sleep;
Our souls and bodies
In Thy love keep.
Waking or sleeping,
Keep us in sight;
Dear, gentle Savior,
Good night, good night.

31. My Savior, hear my prayer
Before I go to rest;
It is Thy little child
That cometh to be blest.

Lord, help me ev'ry day
To love Thee more and more,
To try to do Thy will
Much better than before.

Forgive me all my sin,
And let me sleep this night
In safety and in peace,
Until the morning light. Amen.

32. Dear Lord God, I pray Thee, for Jesus' sake forgive whatever I have done wrong this day, and keep me safe this night. Amen.

33. Lord, bless me! Keep Thou me as Thine;
Lord, make Thy face upon me shine;
Lord, lift Thy countenance on me;
And grant me peace — sweet peace from
    Thee. Amen.

34. I thank Thee, my heavenly Father, through Jesus Christ, Thy dear Son, that Thou hast graciously kept me this day; and I pray Thee that Thou wouldst forgive me all my sins where I have done wrong, and graciously keep me this night. For into Thy hands I commend myself, my body and soul, and all things. Let Thy holy angel be with me, that the wicked Foe may have no power over me. Amen.

Table Prayers

35. Abba, Jesus! Amen.

36. We thank You for our food,
Dear Jesus, kind and good. Amen.

37. God is great, and God is good,
And we thank Him for our food;
By His hand we all are fed;
Give us, Lord, our daily bread. Amen.

38. Come, Lord Jesus, be our Guest,
And let Thy gifts to us be blessed. Amen.

39. Great God, Thou Giver of all good,
Accept our praise and bless our food.
For Jesus' sake. Amen.

40. God bless this food,
And bless us all,
For Jesus' sake. Amen.

41. Be present at our table, Lord;
Be here and everywhere adored.
Thy children bless, and grant that we
May feast in paradise with Thee. Amen.

42. Great God, Thou Giver of all good,
Accept our praise, and bless our food;
Grace, health, and strength, and mercy
    give,
Through Jesus Christ, in whom we live.
    Amen.

[22]

43. Jesus, bless what Thou hast given,
    Feed our souls with bread from heaven;
    Guide and lead us by Thy love
    Until we reach our home above. Amen.

44. For food and all Thy gifts of love,
    We give Thee thanks and praise.
    Look down, O Jesus, from above,
    And bless us all our days. Amen.

45. Lord God, heavenly Father, bless us and these
    Thy gifts, which we receive from Thy boun-
    tiful goodness, through Jesus Christ, our
    Lord. Amen.

46. Grant us Thy grace, O Lord, that, whether
    we eat or drink, or whatever we do, we may
    do it all in Thy name and to Thy glory.
    Amen.

AFTER MEALS

47.   Thank you, Jesus, for this food. Amen.

48.   We thank You, Lord,
      For food and drink,
      Through Jesus Christ. Amen.

49.   For daily food we thank Thee, Lord;
      Be here and everywhere adored. Amen.

50.   Dear Father in heaven, accept our thanks
      for this food and for all Thy blessings,
      through Jesus Christ. Amen.

51.   Bless the Lord, O my soul; and all that is
      within me, bless His holy name. Bless the
      Lord, O my soul, and forget not all His
      benefits. Amen.

52. Oh, give thanks unto the Lord, for He is good; for His mercy endureth forever. Amen.

53. We thank Thee, Lord God, heavenly Father, through Jesus Christ, our Lord, for all Thy benefits, who livest and reignest forever and ever. Amen.

54. We thank Thee, heav'nly Father,
    For ev'ry earthly good,
    For life, and health, and clothing,
    And for our daily food.

    Oh, give us hearts to thank Thee,
    For ev'ry blessing sent,
    And whatsoe'er Thou sendest,
    Make us therewith content. Amen.

55. For health and food, for love and friends.
    For everything Thy goodness sends,
    Father in heaven, we thank Thee. Amen.

56. We thank You, dear Lord Jesus,
That You our Guest have been;
Please stay with us forever,
And save us from all sin. Amen.

57. We thank Thee for these gifts, O Lord;
Now feed our souls, too, with Thy Word.
Amen.

58. The Lord is good to all, and His tender
mercies are over all His works. Bless the
Lord, O my soul, and all that is within me,
bless His holy name. Bless the Lord, O my
soul, and forget not all His benefits. Amen.

59. For food and drink and happy days,
Accept our gratitude and praise;
In serving others, Lord, may we
Express our thankfulness to Thee. Amen.

Prayers in Sickness

60. Lord Jesus, please help me! Amen.

61. Jesus, have mercy on me! Amen.

62. Tender Jesus, meek and mild,
     Look on me, a little child;
     Help me, if it is Thy will,
     To recover from all ill. Amen.

63. Lord Jesus, You were always good
     To everyone in pain;
     Please think of me while I am ill,
     And make me well again. Amen.

64. I am weak, but Thou art mighty.
Help me, Lord. Amen.

65. Dear Jesus, help me believe that all things
work together for good to them that love
God. Amen.

66. Dear Father in heaven, Your child is sick.
Have mercy on me, and if it be Your will,
give me health and strength, and keep me
cheerful, through faith in Jesus, my Lord and
Savior. Amen.

67. Lord Jesus, have mercy on my mother
(father, brother, sister) and make her (him)
well again soon, if it be Your will. You can
do all things; and I know that You love us.
More than anything else, keep us as Your
children, and take us to heaven, for Your
name's sake. Amen.

68. My body Thou hast healed again,
    My spirit now restore;
    Thy praises, Savior, I will sing,
    Thy holy name adore. Amen.

69. Faithful Shepherd, feed me
    In the pastures green;
    Faithful Shepherd, lead me
    Where Thy steps are seen.

    In my sickness help me
    As Thou thinkest best,
    Keep me close beside Thee,
    Give me peace and rest. Amen.

70. Lord, be Thou my loving Guide,
    Lead me every day
    Till I reach Thy home at last,
    Nevermore to stray. Amen.

71. Jesus, help my eyes to see
All the good Thou sendest me.
Jesus, help my ears to hear
Calls for help from far and near.
Jesus, help my feet to go
In the way that Thou wilt show.
Jesus, help my hands to do
All things loving, kind, and true.
Jesus, may I helpful be,
Growing daily more like Thee. Amen.

72. Thy name I praise
In this glad hour,
For Thou hast healed
Me by Thy power;
Lord, let me serve
Thee day by day
And never from
Thy pathway stray. Amen.

For School and Church

73.   Dear Lord Jesus, go with me to school today,
and make me obedient to my teachers. Help
me to learn with pleasure whatever I am
taught, so that I may honor and serve Thee
all my days. Amen.

74.   I was glad when they said unto me,
Let us go into the house of the Lord.

Psalm 122:1

75.   Assembled in our school once more,
O Lord, Thy blessing we implore;
We meet to work, to sing, to pray;
Be with us, then, throughout this day.
Amen.

76. Father, bless our school today;
Be in all we do or say;
Be in ev'ry song we sing;
Ev'ry prayer to Thee we bring.

Jesus, well-beloved Son,
May Thy will by us be done,
Come and meet with us today;
Teach us, Lord, Thyself, we pray. Amen.

77. Since my heavenly Father
Gives me ev'rything,
Lovingly and gladly
Now my gift I bring.

78. Jesus, bless the gifts we bring Thee;
Give them something sweet to do;
May they help someone to love Thee;
Jesus, may we love Thee, too. Amen.

79.   Dear Savior, bless the children
      Who've gathered here today;
      Oh, send Thy Holy Spirit,
      And teach us how to pray.

      Lord, bless the work we're doing,
      Oh, bless our gifts, though small,
      And hear our prayer for Jesus' sake,
      Who died to save us all. Amen.

80.   We thank Thee, Heav'nly Father,
      For all that we have heard;
      Teach us to love our Savior
      And to obey Thy Word. Amen.

81.   Dear Jesus, bless each little child,
      And keep us all, we pray,
      Safe in Thy loving care until
      Another holy day. Amen.

82. Lord, we bring our off'ring;
    Use it that Your Word
    May be told to children
    Who have never heard.

    Some are in our homeland,
    Some across the sea.
    May they learn of Jesus:
    This our prayer shall be. Amen.

83. Father, we thank You for Your Word,
    And for the lessons we have heard;
    Be with us as we homeward go;
    Help us to do the things we know. Amen.

84. Dear Jesus, bless each little child,
    And keep us all, we pray,
    Safe in Your loving care until
    Another holy day. Amen.

General Prayers

85.   Lord, bless the little children
In all the world, we pray;
Help everyone to love Thee,
And keep them in Thy way. Amen.

86.   We thank You, God, for sunshine
And for the gentle rain,
We thank You for the harvest fields
Of waving, golden grain.

We thank You for the flour,
For bread, and all our food;
We thank You, God, for everything;
You are so kind and good. Amen.

87. Lord, teach a little child to pray,
   And, oh, accept my prayer;
   Thou hearest all the words I say,
   For Thou art ev'rywhere.

   A little sparrow cannot fall
   Unnoticed, Lord, by Thee;
   And though I am so young and small,
   Thou canst take care of me.

   Teach me to do whate'er is right,
   And when I sin, forgive;
   And make it always my delight
   To love Thee while I live. Amen.

88. God the Father, bless us;
   God the Son, defend us;
   God the Spirit, keep us
   Now and evermore. Amen.

89. Blest Savior dear, be always near;
   Keep me from evil, harm, and fear. Amen.

90. Jesus, Friend of little children,
Be a Friend to me;
Take my hand, and ever keep me
Close to Thee. Amen.

91. Jesus, tender Savior,
Thou hast died for me;
Make me very thankful
In my heart to Thee.
When the sad, sad story
Of Thy grief I read,
Make me very sorry
For my sins indeed.

Now I know Thou livest
And dost plead for me;
Make me very thankful
In my prayers to Thee.
Soon I hope in glory
At Thy side to stand;
Make me fit to meet Thee
In that happy land! Amen.

92. God made the sun,
And God made the tree;
God made the mountains,
And God made me.

I thank you, O God,
For the sun and the tree,
For making the mountains
And for making me. Amen.

93. Beautiful Savior, King of Creation,
Son of God and Son of Man!
Truly I'd love Thee,
Truly I'd serve Thee,
Light of my soul, my Joy, my Crown.

Fair is the sunshine, Fair is the moonlight,
Bright the sparkling stars on high;
Jesus shines brighter,
Jesus shines purer
Than all the angels in the sky.

94. Jesus, lead me day by day
    Ever in Thine own sweet way;
    Teach me to be pure and true;
    Show me what I ought to do.

    When in danger, make me brave;
    Make me know that Thou dost save;
    Keep me safe by Thy dear side;
    Let me in Thy love abide.

95. Thou who once on mother's knee
    Wast a little child like me,
    When I wake or go to bed,
    Lay Thy hands upon my head;
    Let me feel Thee very near,
    Jesus Christ, my Savior dear. Amen.

96. Praise God, from whom all blessings flow;
    Praise Him, all creatures here below;
    Praise Him above, ye heavenly host:
    Praise Father, Son, and Holy Ghost. Amen.

97. Lord, give Your angels every day
     Command to guide us on our way,
     And bid them every evening keep
     Their watch around us while we sleep.

     So shall no wicked thing draw near,
     To do us harm or cause us fear.
     And we shall dwell, when life is past,
     With angels round Your throne at last.
                                    Amen.

98. Savior, teach me, day by day,
     Love's sweet lesson — to obey;
     Sweeter lesson cannot be,
     Loving Him who first loved me.

     With a child's glad heart of love
     At Thy bidding may I move,
     Prompt to serve and follow Thee,
     Loving Him who first loved me.

Birthday Prayers

99.   Holy Spirit, give me
Now a holy mind;
Make me more like Jesus,
Gentle, pure, and kind.

100.   O Jesus, send Thy tender love
Upon me, please, today.
On this, my birthday, give me grace
A special prayer to say.

Few are my candles, few my years;
So let my promise be
That all the years that I may live
I'll love and worship Thee. Amen.

101. We thank the Lord who kept you
All through the passing year;
He put His arms around you
And gave you health and cheer.

Now we will pray together
That He will keep you still
And make the next year happy
And help you do His will.

102. Teach me to love,
Teach me to pray,
Jesus above,
Teach me Your way.

Tell me how I,
In my own way,
Can, with Your help,
Do good each day.

Prayer for Missions

103. Lord, bless the little children
In all the world, I pray;
Help everyone to love Thee
And do the things You say. Amen.

104. Dear Lord, will You not help us
Obey Your great command,
And send Your blessed Gospel
Abroad through every land?

Lord, bless the work we're doing,
Oh, bless our gifts, though small,
And hear our prayer for Jesus' sake,
Who died to save us all.

A Prayer for You

105. May you live to know and fear God,
Trust and love Him all your days;
Then go dwell forever near Him,
See His face and sing His praise. Amen.